Vikings

Henry Pluckrose
consultant editor

Illustrated by
Ivan Lapper

small WORLD

Evans Brothers Limited

Many hundreds of years ago, the
Vikings lived in Scandinavia.
They were farmers and sailors
and their ships were the
finest in Europe.
But their own land was not good
enough to grow food for everybody.
By the eighth century AD, many
people had decided to seek
their fortunes abroad.
They set sail in search of
slaves, gold and silver.
Later on, they searched for
land in which to settle.
The Vikings attacked countries
all over Europe and people fled
in terror whenever they saw
a Viking ship.

At home, the Vikings lived in
simple one-roomed farmhouses
made of wood, stone and mud.
A fire was kept burning in the
middle of the room. This gave
heat and light. Meals were
cooked in a cauldron hung over the
fire. The Vikings ate vegetables
and stewed meat and drank mead,
a kind of beer made from honey.

The 'Black Houses'
in the Hebrides
are similar to
those the Vikings
lived in.

The Vikings were shipbuilders.
Viking ships were made out of
oak planks joined together with
iron nails.
They had sails as well
as oars.

Viking ships were strong
and fast.
The Vikings were able to sail
great distances in them.

The Vikings were ruled by a king.
Below the king were the
earls, called jarls.
The jarls were very powerful.
They commanded private armies
of free peasants, called karls.
The lowest class was made up
of slaves, called thralls.

The king and his court travelled
from one royal farm to another.
As they feasted, they listened
to poets tell stories about
Viking heroes.

Viking craftsmen were skilled
metal and woodworkers.
On these two pages you can see
some of the beautiful things
they made. Many of these
objects were exported to
foreign countries.
The Vikings exchanged their
ironwork, amber, fur and slaves
for silver, silk and spices.
The silver was made into
coins and jewellery.

Comb

Coins

Here are some Viking objects
made from wood.
Look at the carved decorations.

Ship's figurehead

Trough

Sledge

Bucket

The centre of the Viking trading
empire was the town of
Hedeby in Denmark.
Merchants from Asia and the rest
of Europe gathered here to
buy and sell goods.

By 800 AD there were so many people in the Viking homelands that the land could not support them all. The more adventurous decided to find other countries to settle in. Some Vikings sailed to Britain. The Anglo-Saxons fought fiercely to drive them away, but the Vikings were better soldiers and they conquered much of Britain.

Other Vikings went north to
Iceland and Greenland.
Very few people lived there
so the Vikings were able
to settle.
But Iceland and Greenland were
hard countries to live in.

Both countries were rocky and
covered in ice.
The Vikings could not farm the
land, so they had to live on fish
and whale meat.
Hunting for whales could be
very dangerous.

From Greenland it is only a
short journey to North America.
Some Vikings, led by Leif Eriksson,
tried to settle in the area now
called Newfoundland.
The Vikings called it Vinland.
The Indians who lived in Vinland
were friendly at first but
then fights broke out.
The Indians drove the Vikings
out of Vinland and they
never returned.

This map shows you how far
the Vikings travelled.
They went north to Iceland and
Greenland and south to England
and France (where they settled in
Normandy). They also travelled
to the East for trade.
Some Vikings who went to the
East were soldiers.
A few became the bodyguard
of the Byzantine Emperor, who
had his capital in Constantinople.
They were called the
Varangian Guard. They were
very good soldiers and were
feared all over Europe.

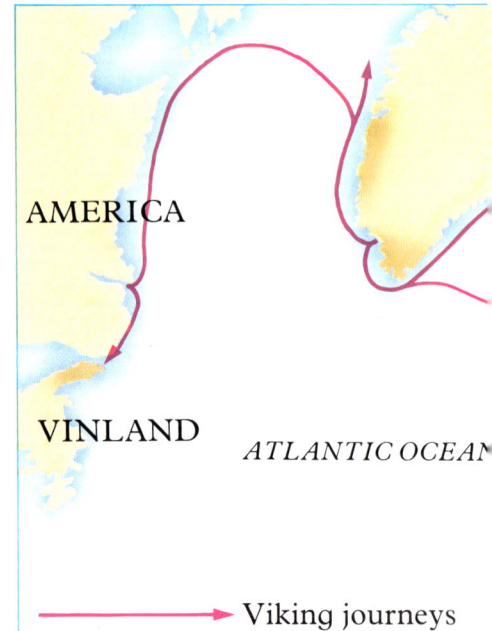

AMERICA

VINLAND

ATLANTIC OCEAN

Viking journeys

Viking treasure

GREENLAND

ICELAND

NORWAY

SWEDEN

DENMARK

Hedeby

POLAND

RUSSIA

IRELAND

ENGLAND

GERMANY

BLACK SEA

FRANCE

ITALY

Constantinople

SPAIN

MEDITERRANEAN SEA

The Vikings worshipped many
gods. Two of the most
important were Odin and Thor.
Vikings believed in a heaven
called Valhalla. This was
where the gods lived and where
brave warriors went after death.
When a rich Viking died, he might
be burned in his ship or buried
in a wood-lined chamber with all
his belongings beside him.

A rich Viking
would be buried
with all his
possessions
beside him.

As the Vikings
settled in other
countries, they
adopted the
traditions and
religions of their
new home.
By the twelfth
century, all
Scandinavia had
become Christian
and the great
Viking age in
Europe was over.

You can still see
this early
wooden Christian
church in Norway.

Today we can not only read
Viking legends, we can still see
many of the beautiful things the
Vikings made. Our language
contains many words which come
from those first spoken by the
Vikings over a thousand years ago.

Index